New York Mets Trivia

The Silver Anniversary Book

by
Mike Getz

Quinlan Press
Boston

Copyright © 1987 by
Mike Getz
All rights reserved,
including the right of reproduction
in whole or in part in any form.
Published by Quinlan Press
131 Beverly Street
Boston, MA 02114

Cover design by Christopher Bergan

Library of Congress
Catalog Card Number 87-60165
ISBN 0-933341-81-4

Printed in the United States of America
March 1987

Dedicated to Casey and Gil

Mike Getz, a freelance writer, has been an ardent sports fan for over forty years. His contributions have appeared in a number of magazines and newspapers, including *Baseball Digest, Baseball Bulletin* and *Diamond Report.* As a member of the Society for American Baseball Research, Getz was one of the chief organizers of the first annual New York SABR Regional held at Shea Stadium in 1984. His previous books include *Baseball's 3,000-Hit Men* and *New York Yankees Trivia.* His many radio appearances include "The Art Rust Show" (WABC) and "In the Public Interest" (WHN). Mr. Getz lives with his wife, Virginia, and teenage son, Vincent, in Brooklyn, New York.

To those who generously devoted their time and energy to this project and others who provided much needed advice and encouragement, acknowledgements are due: the New York Mets, Ross Adell, Victor Amoros, Donald Angelo, Sam Brodkin, Dick Cohen, Dennis D'Agostino, Mickey Dilworth, Scott Flatow, Vincent Getz, John Grabowski, Virginia Getz, Miriam Lamb, John Looney, Marcia Mammano, Vincent Pellegrini, Bill Rehak, Joan Rehak, Paul Szeflinski, and Larry Curcio and Kevin Stevens of Quinlan Press.

CONTENTS

HISTORY
  Questions 1
  Answers 13

MEMORABLE GAMES
  Questions 23
  Answers 31

AT THE PLATE AND ON THE BASES
  Questions 37
  Answers 53

PHOTOGRAPHS
  Questions 65
  Answers 101

ON THE MOUND
  Questions 105
  Answers 119

ON THE FIELD
  Questions 129
  Answers 133

TRADES
  Questions 137
  Answers 143

MANAGERS AND COACHES
  Questions 149
  Answers 153

MISCELLANEOUS
  Questions 157
  Answers 173

History

1. Name four former Mets players who were elected to the Hall of Fame.

2. How many games did the Mets lose in their first season?

3. Which four Mets won Rookie of the Year awards?

4. How many games did the Mets win in their first world championship year (1969)?

5. Who was the lone regular to bat over .300 in the first year of the Mets' existence (1962)?

History—Questions

6. In the first year of play at Shea Stadium (1964), which two regulars reached the .300 mark?

7. In 1963 who competed with Pete Rose for Rookie of the Year?

8. Who won the "Comeback Player of the Year" award for 1969?

9. Who was the first free agent signed by the Mets from the re-entry draft?

10. Who was the winningest pitcher in the Mets' first year?

11. What is the Mets' biggest winning streak?

12. How many games did the first Mets team win?

13. When the Mets began in 1962, how many games did the team lose before they won once?

14. Which pitcher got credit for the Mets' first win?

15. Which team was the first to lose to the Mets?

16. Name the three players who reached 1,000 hits as Mets?

History—Questions

17. Who was the main man responsible for bringing National League baseball back to New York?

18. Who was the only player to reach 2,000 total bases during his career as a Met?

19. What was the Mets' record in the Polo Grounds in 1962?

20. Who was the first player ever to sign a Mets contract?

21. Who was the first Mets player to be drafted?

22. Who was the Mets' original mascot?

23. Who was the first Met to hit a home run in his first major league at-bat?

24. Who was the first player ever to bat for the Mets?

25. Name the four ex-Brooklyn Dodgers to appear in the original Mets' opening-day starting lineup.

26. Who was the first player ever to drive in a run against the Mets?

27. Which player was the first ever to drive in a run for the Mets?

History—Questions

28. Who was the first player to score a run for the Mets?

29. Who was the first player to hit a home run for the Mets?

30. Who was the Mets first relief pitcher?

31. Who was the first Met to hit three home runs in one game?

32. Who made the first hit in Mets history?

33. How many opening-day losses did the Mets suffer before winning one?

34. Who was the first Met to start in an All-Star game?

35. Name the first Met to appear in an All-Star game.

36. Who was the lone Met in the 1963 All-Star Game?

37. Identify the Met who narrowly missed Rookie of the Year honors in 1977, although he played only from June on.

38. How many times did the Mets finish tenth?

39. How many times did the Mets finish third in their first 20 years?

History—Questions

40. How many times have the Mets finished second?

41. In 1963 who ran backwards around the bases after hitting his 100th home run?

42. When the Mets finally won a home opener, who was the winning pitcher and what was the score?

43. Who was voted Most Valuable Met of the first season?

44. Who was the first Met to pitch a shutout?

45. Name the first Met to hit for the cycle (single, double, triple and home run in one game).

46. Who hit the first home run in Shea Stadium?

47. What was the date of the Mets' first official game?

48. In 1962 what was the price of a bleacher seat for a Mets game at the Polo Grounds?

49. Who hit the first Mets home run in the Polo Grounds?

50. What league records were set when the Pirates defeated the Mets 4-3 on April 22, 1962?

History—Questions

51. Who was the first to pitch a no-hitter against the Mets?

52. How many games did the Mets win (out of nine) in Cincinnati in 1962?

53. What was the original name picked for Shea Stadium?

54. Who was voted Most Popular Met of the first season: Richie Ashburn, Gil Hodges or Marv Throneberry?

55. What was the "Thursday Jinx"?

56. In which season did the Mets lose 22 road games in a row—1962, 1963 or 1964?

57. Name the three Mets who homered one after another for the first time in the team's history.

58. Who hit the last home run in the Polo Grounds?

59. Who was the starting pitcher for the Mets in the first game played at Shea Stadium?

60. Who hit the first Mets homer in Shea Stadium?

61. Who was the first Met to get five hits in one game?

History—Questions

62. Name the last man to bat in the Polo Grounds.

63. Who was voted Most Valuable Met in both 1963 and 1964?

64. Who hit the first grand-slam homer for the Mets: Jim Hickman, Ron Hunt, Rod Kanehl or Frank Thomas?

65. Who was chosen Most Valuable Player in the 1969 World Series: Tommie Agee, Donn Clendenon, Cleon Jones or Ron Swoboda?

66. Who made the first Mets hit in Shea Stadium: Richie Ashburn, Gus Bell, Tim Harkness or Ron Hunt?

67. Who was the Mets' first-ever selection in the (college-high school) free-agent draft?

68. Name the three starting pitchers with a combined 40-0 record against the Mets by mid-1965.

69. How long did it take for the Mets to reach the .500 mark for the very first time?

70. Who hit the first pinch-hit grand-slam homer in Mets history?

71. Who was the first starting pitcher in Mets

History—Questions

history to finish a season with a winning record?

72. Who holds the Mets club record for runs scored in one season?

73. How many players did the Mets use in setting a National League record in 1967: 45, 48, 51 or 54?

74. How did the Mets do in their last 50 games in 1969?

75. In which year did the Mets have winning streaks of seven, nine, ten and eleven games?

76. Whose base hit put the Mets into first place for the first time in their history?

77. In what year did the Mets win the opening game of the season for the first time?

78. Who was the winning pitcher in the above game?

79. Who held the Mets hitting-streak record from 1962 to 1970?

80. How many runs did the Mets score in the three-game playoff against the Braves in 1969?

History—Questions

81. Name the rookie pitcher who won the game that clinched the Mets' Eastern Division title in 1969?

82. Who "hammered" the ball in spring training of 1972 and was voted top rookie in camp?

83. What was the Mets' record in the second half of 1973?

84. After the 1980 season, who had beaten the Mets more often than any other pitcher?

85. Who made more hits in one season than any other Mets pitcher?

86. On the morning of July 4, 1973, what was the position of the New York Mets in the standings?

87. With 32 games remaining in the 1973 schedule, how did the Mets rise from last place to the division title?

88. What was the Reds' highest run-scoring total against the Mets in the 1973 playoff?

89. How many Mets played on both the 1969 and 1973 pennant winners?

90. In which years did the Yankees play their home games in Shea Stadium?

9

History—Questions

91. Who was the starting pitcher in the first Mets game in the Polo Grounds?

92. In 1970 who drove in seven runs in one game for a club record: Tommie Agee, Cleon Jones, Donn Clendenon or Ed Kranepool?

93. In 1976 who drove in eight runs in one game to break the club record?

94. Who was the first Met to hit an inside-the-park home run in Shea Stadium?

95. How many runs did the Mets score in their biggest inning?

96. In 1980 who broke Bud Harrelson's lifetime team stolen base record?

97. Who drew the largest season crowds in their best season: the Yankees, the Brooklyn Dodgers, the New York Giants or the Mets?

98. In 1982 who broke the Mets' record for stolen bases in a season?

99. In 1983 who had eight straight pinch hits to tie a 25-year-old major league record?

100. From 1975 to 1983 how many times did the Mets lose on opening day?

History—Questions

101. Which four Mets were chosen for the 1984 All-Star Game?

102. Name the three broadcasters who were elected to the Mets Hall of Fame in 1984.

103. Whose National League record for strikeouts by a rookie pitcher was broken by Dwight Gooden?

104. Whose major league record for strikeouts by a rookie was broken by Gooden?

105. What is the record for most hits by a Mets team in a single game?

106. In 1985 the Mets had two starting players elected to the All-Star team. Who were they?

107. Whose club record for shutouts did Gooden break when he posted his eighth shutout in one season?

108. Which team record did the Mets reach for the third time in 1986?

109. Which five Mets were chosen for the 1986 All-Star team? Who played and who didn't?

110. Who were the first two players elected to the Mets Hall of Fame?

History—Questions

111. True or false: Mets attendance in 1986 was the best in New York baseball history.

112. True or false: Gary Carter broke Rusty Staub's single-season Met record for RBIs.

113. Who set a Mets record by pitching in 75 games in 1986?

114. How many regular-season games were won by the 1986 Mets?

115. In which categories did the 1986 Mets lead the league?

116. Who was chosen Most Valuable Player of the 1986 World Series?

Answers

1. Yogi Berra, Willie Mays, Duke Snider and Warren Spahn

2. 120

3. Tom Seaver in 1967, Jon Matlack in 1972, Darryl Strawberry in 1983 and Dwight Gooden in 1984

4. 100 regular-season games

5. Richie Ashburn batted .306.

6. Ron Hunt hit .303; Joe Christopher batted .300.

7. Ron Hunt

History—Answers

8. Tommie Agee

9. Tom Hausman

10. Roger Craig had ten wins.

11. 11 games in a row

12. 40

13. Nine

14. Jay Hook

15. The Pittsburgh Pirates

16. Ed Kranepool, Cleon Jones and Bud Harrelson

17. Bill Shea

18. Ed Kranepool

19. 22 wins and 58 losses

20. Ted Lepcio, a ten-year veteran

21. Hobie Landrith

22. A beagle named Homer

23. Benny Ayala

24. Richie Ashburn

14

History—Answers

25. Gil Hodges at first, Charlie Neal at second, Don Zimmer at third and Roger Craig on the mound

26. Stan Musial

27. Charlie Neal

28. Richie Ashburn

29. Gil Hodges

30. Bob Moorhead

31. Jim Hickman

32. Gus Bell

33. Eight

34. Ron Hunt (1964)

35. Richie Ashburn

36. Duke Snider

37. Steve Henderson

38. Five

39. Five

40. Twice; in 1984 and 1985

History—Answers

41. Jim Piersall

42. Jerry Koosman beat the Giants, 3-0.

43. Richie Ashburn

44. Al Jackson

45. Jim Hickman (August 7, 1963)

46. Willie Stargell's homer was also the first hit in Shea Stadium.

47. April 11, 1962. The original opener was rained out the day before.

48. 75 cents

49. Frank Thomas

50. The Mets, by losing their ninth in a row, tied the National League record for most consecutive losses at the start of a season. The Pirates, by winning the contest, tied the modern major league record of a ten-game winning streak at the start of a season.

51. Sandy Koufax (June 30, 1962)

52. None

53. Flushing Meadows Stadium

History—Answers

54. Gil Hodges

55. From the time Mets play began, the team did not win a game on a Thursday for over a year (16 Thursday losses in a row).

56. 1963

57. Frank Thomas, Charlie Neal and Gil Hodges (1962)

58. Jim Hickman

59. Jack Fisher

60. Ron Hunt

61. Dick Smith

62. Ted Schreiber

63. Ron Hunt

64. Rod Kanehl

65. Donn Clendenon

66. Tim Harkness

67. Les Rohr

68. Juan Marichal, 14-0; Larry Jackson, 13-0; and Sandy Koufax, 13-0

History—Answers

69. After four full seasons (1962-1965), the Mets reached the .500 mark for the first time with a 1-1 record in April, 1966. It was their 648th game.

70. Bob ("Hawk") Taylor

71. Dennis Ribant

72. Tommie Agee—107

73. 54

74. They played .760 ball, winning 38 and losing only 12! The club went from 62 wins and 50 losses to 100 wins and 62 losses.

75. In 1969 the Mets had four winning streaks of seven or more games. In September the club won ten straight at one point and nine in a row up to the last game of the season. They then lost a meaningless game to the Cubs before winning seven out of eight in postseason play.

76. Ken Boswell drove in the winning run in a 12-inning game to move the Mets past Chicago in September 1969.

77. In 1970, after eight consecutive opening day losses, the Mets defeated the Pirates 5-3 in 11 innings.

History—Answers

78. Ron Taylor

79. Frank Thomas—18 straight

80. 27 runs in three games

81. Gary Gentry

82. John Milner

83. In 1973, after winning only 34 games while dropping 46 during the first half-season, the Mets won 48 and lost only 33 in the second half.

84. Bob Gibson beat the Mets 28 times during his career.

85. Dwight Gooden socked 21 hits in 1985 for a new club record.

86. Dead last—11 games behind. The Mets eventually dropped 12 games behind (15 in the win column) before climbing to the top.

87. The Mets won 23 and lost 9.

88. Two runs each in games one, three, four and five

89. 11 Mets played on both pennant winners.

History—Answers

90. 1974 and 1975

91. Sherman (Roadblock) Jones

92. Donn Clendenon

93. Dave Kingman

94. Ron Hunt

95. The Mets scored ten runs in one inning in a game against the Cincinnati Reds in June 1979.

96. Lee Mazzilli

97. The Mets!

98. Mookie Wilson

99. Rusty Staub

100. None

101. Darryl Strawberry, Dwight Gooden, Jesse Orosco and Keith Hernandez

102. Ralph Kiner, Lindsey Nelson and Bob Murphy

103. Grover Cleveland Alexander

104. Herb Score

History—Answers

105. 28

106. Gary Carter and Darryl Strawberry

107. Jerry Koosman (1968) and Jon Matlack (1974)

108. The Mets won 11 games in a row.

109. Gary Carter, Sid Fernandez, Dwight Gooden, Keith Hernandez and Darryl Strawberry were chosen for the All-Star team. Each one appeared in the game. Manager Dave Johnson was also selected as a coach.

110. Bud Harrelson and Rusty Staub

111. True—2,762,417 paid.

112. False—Carter tied Staub with 105 RBIs.

113. Roger McDowell

114. 108

115. ERA—3.11, batting—.263 and runs scored—783

116. Ray Knight

Memorable Games

1. Who was the winning pitcher in the final playoff game against the Braves in 1969?

2. Who hit three home runs in a game against the Los Angeles Dodgers in 1980?

3. Who was the winning pitcher in the final game of the 1969 World Series?

4. Name the pitcher who struck out 19 Mets in a game, but lost the game.

5. When Steve Carlton struck out 19 Mets in one game, who beat him with two home runs?

Memorable Games—Questions

6. Who beat Juan Marichal with a homer in the 14th inning in a 1-0 win for the Mets?

7. Who fanned Carl Yastrzemski for the final out in the 1968 All-Star Game to preserve a 1-0 win for the National League?

8. After Jim Maloney no-hit the Mets for 10 innings, who homered in the 11th to beat him?

9. Who fanned five batters in 2 innings in the 1968 All-Star Game?

10. Who pitched 10 scoreless innings during a 24-inning game against the Astros?

11. Who won the 23-inning game between the Mets and the San Francisco Giants?

12. Who was the losing pitcher when Jim Bunning pitched his perfect game against the Mets (1964)?

13. Name the pitcher who allowed only two hits (both homers to Hank Aaron) and lost 3-2.

14. Who was the player to get both hits when Gary Gentry pitched a two-hitter?

15. On September 24, 1975, who broke up Seaver's bid for a no-hitter in the 9th inning?

Memorable Games—Questions

16. What was the score of the wild game in which Dick Smith got five hits?

17. Who won the first game played between the Mets and the Yankees?

18. When Al Jackson one-hit the Houston Colts, who singled in the 1st inning for Houston's only hit of the game?

19. How did the Mets beat the Dodgers 10-4 with only four hits?

20. Who shut out the Mets for the last 10 innings of the 23-inning game against the Giants?

21. This man pitched a perfect game against the Mets. It was the first perfect game in the National League in 84 years. Name him.

22. In 1965 which two pitching greats were engaged in a 1-0 game, decided when one of them homered?

23. Name the opposing pitcher who threw a no-hitter for 10 innings, struck out 18 batters and lost the game to the Mets.

24. Who homered to ruin a Koufax no-hitter?

25. Who hit a double, two triples and a homer in a game against the Pirates?

Memorable Games—Questions

26. Who hit two homers for the Mets in a game in which Willie McCovey hit three?

27. Who pitched 15 innings in a 0-0 game?

28. Which player made both hits when Bo Belinsky pitched a two-hitter against the Mets?

29. Which Met, while playing shortstop, knocked in the last six runs of a game with two three-run homers?

30. Do you remember the first game played between the Mets and the Montreal Expos? It was the opening game of the 1969 season. Who won? What was the score?

31. What was the score of the great 18-inning pitching duel between the Mets and the Phillies?

32. Which two players hit bases-loaded homers in the same inning against the Mets? Hint: they were Astros.

33. In September 1969 the Miracle Mets won a doubleheader from the Pirates by identical 1-0 scores. Name the pitchers who won these games and also drove in the winning runs.

34. Who was thrown out of Game 4 of the

Memorable Games—Questions

1969 World Series by umpire Shag Crawford?

35. Who spoiled Gary Gentry's no-hit bid against the Cubs?

36. Who ruined Gary Gentry's second no-hit bid with a triple?

37. Who had a five-hit, five-RBI game against the Giants in 1970?

38. Who was taken out of the game in the 8th inning while pitching a no-hitter against the Mets?

39. Who stole home in the bottom of the 10th inning to beat the Dodgers 2-1?

40. In 1970 who ruined Ferguson Jenkins's no-hit bid with two doubles on the last day of the season?

41. What happened in Willie Mays's first game as a Met?

42. Who was the winning pitcher in the 1972 All-Star Game?

43. How many home runs were hit in the game in which the Mets and Cubs broke the National League record?

44. When Jon Matlack pitched a one-hitter against the Houston Astros, who got the only hit?

Memorable Games—Questions

45. Who made the only two hits off Jon Matlack in the second playoff game with the Reds in 1973?

46. How many batters did the Mets send to the plate in the 25-inning game against the Cardinals?

47. Whom did the Mets oppose in the longest night game in baseball history?

48. Who homered in the bottom of the 14th inning for a 1-0 victory over the Dodgers: Tommie Agee, Dave Kingman, John Milner or Rusty Staub?

49. Which Mets leadoff man socked a single, double, triple and homer in a game against the Cubs: Tommie Agee, Bud Harrelson, Mike Phillips or Del Unser?

50. In 1980 who pitched a two-hitter for the Mets — and lost?

51. Whose 9th-inning, two-out, two-strike homer beat the Dodgers 7-6 after the Mets trailed 6-0?

52. In 1982 whose no-hit bid was ruined with two out in the 8th inning?

53. Who hit the ball that disappeared in the fog and ended the ballgame?

Memorable Games—Questions

54. Who pitched a 10-inning one-hitter for the Mets in 1982?

55. When the Mets lost the 1984 opening game at Shea Stadium 10-0 to the Expos, who hit a grand-slam homer off Ron Darling?

56. How many hits did the Mets get in Sid Fernandez's first start?

57. Whose first home run in over two years broke up a 0-0 extra-inning game?

58. When the Mets had the bases loaded with nobody out in the 1st inning, and a 3-0 count on Gary Carter, who stopped them cold and shut them out?

59. What was the score of the 33-run game between the Mets and the Phillies?

60. What was the final score of the July 4 fireworks night game in which Dwight Gooden started, Ron Darling finished, McDowell, Leach, Orosco and Sisk relieved and Gorman won?

61. Who had five hits in the July 4 game?

62. Who hit for the cycle in the July 4 game?

Memorable Games—Questions

63. In a 1986 game, whose pinch-hit grand-slam homer in the bottom of the 11th inning beat the Phillies 8-4?

64. In 1986, when the Astros beat the Mets 1-0 in the first NLCS game, how did Houston score their run?

65. Who relieved Bob Ojeda in Game 2 of the NLCS after he had given up ten hits?

66. When Gary Carter singled in the 12th inning to win Game 5, 2-1, who scored the winning run?

67. What was unusual about the opening game of the 1986 World Series (won by the Red Sox, 1-0)?

68. Who had four hits for the Mets in Game 3?

69. In Game 4, who hit the ball that bounced out of Dwight Evans's glove for a home run?

70. In Game 6, trailing 5-3, with two out and nobody on base in the bottom of the 10th, which three Mets singled to keep the game (and the World Series) alive?

71. In Game 7, who pitched magnificently in relief, allowing no hits or runs in 2⅓ innings?

Answers

1. Nolan Ryan

2. Claudell Washington

3. Jerry Koosman

4. Steve Carlton

5. Ron Swoboda

6. Tommie Agee

7. Jerry Koosman

8. Johnny Lewis

Memorable Games—Answers

9. Tom Seaver

10. Tom Seaver

11. The Giants won 8-6.

12. Tracy Stallard

13. Willard Hunter (June 20, 1962)

14. Bobby Bonds

15. Joe Wallis, a rookie

16. Mets 19, Cubs 1

17. The Mets won the exhibition contest 4-3.

18. Joe Amalfitano

19. 16 Mets walked

20. Gaylord Perry

21. Jim Bunning (1964)

22. Jim Bunning (Phillies) defeated Warren Spahn (Mets) 1-0 on Bunning's homer.

23. Jim Maloney

24. Jim Hickman (June 20, 1965)

Memorable Games—Answers

25. Joe Christopher

26. Al Luplow

27. Rob Gardner

28. Tommy Davis

29. Jerry Buchek

30. Montreal won 11-10.

31. A 0-0 tie after 18 innings

32. Denis Menke and Jim Wynn hit grand-slammers in the same inning against the Mets (1969).

33. In the first game of the doubleheader, Jerry Koosman pitched a 1-0 shutout and drove in the only run. In the second game, Don Cardwell also pitched a 1-0 shutout and drove in the only run.

34. Orioles manager Earl Weaver

35. Ernie Banks's 8th-inning single was the only hit off Gentry.

36. Roberto Clemente

37. Joe Foy

Memorable Games—Answers

38. Clay Kirby of the Padres was removed for a pinch-hitter in the bottom of the 8th inning. At the time, he was pitching a no-hitter but trailing the Mets 1-0. The Mets won the game 3-0.

39. Tommie Agee

40. Ken Singleton

41. Mays's homer beat his former Giant teammates 5-4.

42. Tug McGraw

43. The Cubs (7) and the Mets (4) hit 11 homers in one game.

44. Tommy Helms

45. Andy Kosco

46. 89

47. The Mets lost to the Cardinals 4-3 in 25 innings in September 1974.

48. Dave Kingman

49. Mike Phillips

50. Ray Burris two-hit San Diego and lost 1-0.

Memorable Games—Answers

51. Steve Henderson

52. Pat Zachry

53. Joel Youngblood's drive fell for a triple and the game was called immediately after (a tie).

54. Terry Leach

55. Gary Carter

56. 22

57. Wally Backman's

58. LaMarr Hoyt, the San Diego Padres

59. Phillies 26, Mets 7

60. Mets 16, Braves 13, in 19 innings

61. Gary Carter

62. Keith Hernandez

63. Tim Teufel

64. On a home run by Glenn Davis

65. No one. Ojeda pitched the complete game, allowing only one run.

Memorable Games—Answers

66. Wally Backman

67. Both the Mets and Red Sox had only singles.

68. Len Dykstra

69. Len Dykstra

70. Gary Carter, Kevin Mitchell and Ray Knight

71. Sid Fernandez

At the Plate and on the Bases

1. Which Mets player tied a major league record by hitting three triples in one game?

2. Who held the Mets' one-season home run record before Dave Kingman?

3. Who was the Mets' home run and RBI leader in their first world championship year (1969)?

4. What Mets player finished third in batting to Pete Rose and Roberto Clemente in 1969?

5. In his first full season with the Mets, this

At the Plate and on the Bases—Questions

veteran socked 22 home runs and drove in 97 runs. Name him.

6. Who set a major league record with a .486 pinch-hit average in 1974?

7. How many home runs did Marvelous Marv Throneberry hit in his first year with the Mets?

8. Who socked three homers in the 1969 World Series?

9. Who hit two homers in the 1973 World Series?

10. Who led all players in hits in the 1973 World Series?

11. Which left-handed hitter socked 23 homers in 1973?

12. Which left-handed slugger led the club in home runs four times?

13. Who led all players in hits in the 1969 World Series?

14. How many RBIs did Richie Hebner get in his season with the Mets?

15. Who was the team RBI leader for the 1973 pennant winners?

At the Plate and on the Bases—Questions

16. Who was the team batting leader for the 1973 pennant winners?

17. Name the only player to steal a base for the Mets in World Series competition prior to 1986.

18. Which Met stole 41 bases in 1980?

19. Who holds the team record for getting one or more hits in the most consecutive games? How many?

20. Name the player with the highest one-season batting average in Mets history.

21. What still-active player leads the Mets in lifetime triples?

22. What player retired with 999 hits?

23. Name the Mets RBI record-holder for one season.

24. Who stole more bases in one season than any other National League catcher?

25. Who had more doubles lifetime: Mets announcer and Hall of Famer Ralph Kiner or Ed Kranepool?

26. How many bases did Frank Taveras steal in his best major league season?

At the Plate and on the Bases—Questions

27. Who hit three pinch homers for the Mets in 1978?

28. Who socked 24 homers, stole 31 bases and scored 107 runs for the Mets in 1970?

29. Who batted over 500 times in 1974 and struck out only 14 times?

30. How many hits did Don Hahn get in the 1973 World Series?

31. Name the Mets rookie who batted .302 in 1975.

32. Which Mets infielder batted .302 in 1977?

33. Who batted .538 in the 1969 playoffs against the Atlanta Braves?

34. Who socked 37 doubles for the Mets in 1979?

35. Which Met had the most hits in 1981?

36. Who had an 18-game hitting streak in 1980?

37. Which Met was once the toughest player in the league to strike out?

38. Which Met hit six homers in three games?

39. Who scored from second a wild pitch?

At the Plate and on the Bases—Questions

40. In the last game of 1981, which rookie tried to score from second base on an infield groundout?

41. Who hit .309 and .307 in his first two years with the Mets?

42. Which Met once hit 66 home runs in one season as a minor leaguer?

43. Which Met batted over 700 times in one season (including walks)?

44. Which Mets catcher hit into a triple play?

45. What did Ed Kranepool bat in his best season?

46. Who had a combined five-year pinch-hitting average of .396 during the second half of his career?

47. Who broke Tommie Agee's one-season club record for stolen bases?

48. Who was still the team's lifetime leader in runs scored through 1985?

49. Who stole seven bases in a 7-inning game in the minors?

50. Which Met led the league in pinch-hit appearances in 1973?

At the Plate and on the Bases — Questions

51. Who was the leading pinch-hitter in the National League in 1976?

52. Which Mets star batted right-handed and threw left-handed?

53. Who set a National League record by hitting into four double plays in one game?

54. In his first game as a Met, this left-handed-hitting outfielder socked a game-winning home run. Name him.

55. Who socked 191 hits in one season for the Mets?

56. Who had more homers as a Met: Gil Hodges or Duke Snider?

57. Which player hit the 400th home run of his career when he was a Met?

58. Which Met had identical home run and RBI totals in 1966 and 1968?

59. How many bases-loaded homers did Gil Hodges hit?

60. Who holds the Mets record for home runs by a rookie?

61. Which Mets power hitter smashed 30 homers as a Pirates rookie?

At the Plate and on the Bases—Questions

62. Which Mets reserve led the league in pinch hits in 1967? Hint: he batted .348 that year.

63. This part-time catcher batted .311 for the Mets in 1964. He also caught for the Cards, Pirates, Padres, Cubs and Dodgers. Name him.

64. As a 33-year-old in his second year with the Mets, this player socked 15 homers. Name this infielder.

65. In 1967 which Met hit the only New York homer in Dodger Stadium?

66. Who smacked five straight hits off Juan Marichal?

67. Who appeared in 16 games for the Mets in 1967, four games in 1969, and wound up with final season averages of .323 and .300 respectively?

68. Which Met hit the first home run of his career inside the park?

69. Who led the original Mets club in stolen bases? How many?

70. Which Mets second baseman led the league in pinch hits in 1966?

At the Plate and on the Bases—Questions

71. Who hit the first Mets homer in the Astrodome?

72. Which Met had a four-hit game in the 1973 World Series?

73. Who had a five-RBI game in the 1973 World Series?

74. Which Met had the longest hitting streak in the majors in 1975?

75. Who batted 41 times for the Mets in 1975, but failed to get a base hit?

76. In 1969 how many times did Tommie Agee lead off a ballgame with a home run?

77. How many homers did second baseman Jerry Buchek hit in 1967?

78. This original Met socked 60 home runs during his career with the club, then another 97 as a Cub. Name him.

79. What major achievements did Richie Ashburn and Duke Snider reach while they were members of the Mets?

80. When Richie Ashburn homered twice in one game, what personal home-run record did he set?

At the Plate and on the Bases—Questions

81. Who hit two homers for the Mets in each game on August 1, 2 and 3, 1962?

82. Who missed first and second base on his way to a triple?

83. Who was hit by a pitch twice in one inning?

84. This Mets first baseman homered in the 16th inning to defeat the Braves. Earlier in the season (1963), he hit a grand-slammer in the 14th inning to beat the Cubs. Name the popular player.

85. Who stole home as part of a triple steal against the Phillies: Bud Harrelson, Lee Mazzilli, Dick Smith or Mookie Wilson?

86. Which player made 500 or more hits with each of four different teams?

87. In 1964 which Met tied a National League record with five straight extra-base hits: Joe Christopher, Jim Hickman, Ron Hunt or Frank Thomas?

88. Which member of the 1965 pitching staff holds the record for the most lifetime homers by a National League pitcher?

89. Whose first two major league hits were homers?

45

At the Plate and on the Bases—Questions

90. Who reached base 18 out of 19 times against the Giants?

91. Before he played for the Mets, who once hit three home runs in four innings: George Foster, Dave Kingman, Willie Mays or Art Shamsky?

92. In 1978 who socked a pinch-hit grand-slam homer against the Montreal Expos: Ken Henderson, Steve Henderson, Lee Mazzilli or Joel Youngblood?

93. Which major lifetime achievement did Ken Boyer reach while he was a Mets player?

94. Which Mets batters ruined no-hitters twice?

95. What was Al Weis's batting average in the 1969 World Series?

96. Which Met reached base 10 times in one afternoon?

97. Who made seven straight singles against the Cardinals?

98. Who got konked on the head by a throw from the outfield while running out a triple (in his first starting game)?

At the Plate and on the Bases—Questions

99. In 1972 which Mets rookie had a five-hit game against the Cardinals?

100. Who hit five pinch-hit home runs for the Mets?

101. Who tied a record with three pinch-hits in a World Series?

102. Which personal hitting records did Cleon Jones and Felix Millan achieve just one day apart?

103. Who hit six homers in the last ten games of 1973?

104. In how many consecutive games did Joe Torre bat safely for the Mets in 1975?

105. Who was the second Met to belt three homers in one game?

106. Which Met went four-for-four and was taken out of the game for a pinch-hitter?

107. Who made his Mets debut with a single, two doubles and a home run?

108. Whose two-base hit prevented Steve Carlton from pitching a no-hitter against the Mets?

109. Who beat out a grounder to spoil a no-hit bid by John Denny of the Cardinals?

At the Plate and on the Bases—Questions

110. Who led the Mets in RBIs in 1977 although he did not play until June?

111. Who batted over 400 times for the Mets without hitting into a double play?

112. When Ed Kranepool retired, where did he rank on the all-time pinch-hit list?

113. When Dave Kingman hit three home runs in a game against the Mets, what was the final score?

114. Name the first two Mets to score five runs in one game.

115. Which Mets previously hit over 50 homers in a season with their former clubs?

116. Who was the first batter to get four hits in one game off Fernando Valenzuela?

117. Who had the lowest batting average while winning a home run championship?

118. Who led Mets pinch-hitters with a .313 batting average in 1982?

119. In 1983 who homered for the Mets in his first major league at-bat?

120. Who could be counted on to pinch-hit, steal a base, play second, third, shortstop or the outfield?

At the Plate and on the Bases—Questions

121. Who borrowed Keith Hernandez's bat and drove in four runs with a single, two doubles and a home run?

122. In 1984 who stepped up to the plate for the first time in two years and socked a pinch-hit double?

123. Who was the victim of Rusty Staub's first homer?

124. What did Gary Carter do his first time at bat as a Met?

125. How did Carter end his first game as a Met?

126. Who was the first major league hitter in 1985 to get five hits in a game?

127. Which team was the victim of Darryl Strawberry's first grand-slammer?

128. Whose line drive was called foul by the umpire at first base and then called a home run by the umpire behind the plate?

129. In 1985 who had more career grand-slam homers (12) than any active National Leaguer?

130. Who was the victim of Nolan Ryan's 4,000th strikeout?

At the Plate and on the Bases—Questions

131. Who hit a grand-slam homer, a three-run homer and a triple in one game?

132. Who had three five-hit games for the Mets in 1985?

133. Which two Mets hit three homers in a game during 1985?

134. In 1985 who ranked third on the Mets behind Hernandez and Carter in official at-bats?

135. Which Met was the first to have a five-hit game in 1986?

136. Who surprisingly hit six home runs during the first month of the season, after hitting only six homers in the entire previous season?

137. Who started his first game in the major leagues by getting three consecutive singles and the game-winning RBI?

138. In 1986 which two Mets rookies hit their first career homers in the same game?

139. Who hit his first homer of the year on his birthday in late September?

140. Who was the first player to have two 100-RBI seasons as a Met?

At the Plate and on the Bases—Questions

141. Who was the only Met to bat over .300 in the 1986 NLCS against the Astros?

142. What was the Mets team batting average in the 1986 NLCS?

143. Who got his first hit of the season in the 1986 World Series?

144. Who led Met players in hits and RBIs in that World Series?

Answers

1. Doug Flynn on August 5, 1980, at Montreal

2. Frank Thomas—34 in 1962

3. Tommie Agee—26 homers; 76 RBIs

4. Cleon Jones—.340

5. Donn Clendenon

6. Ed Kranepool—17 hits in 35 times at bat

7. 16

At the Plate and on the Bases—Answers

8. Donn Clendenon

9. Wayne Garrett

10. Rusty Staub—11 hits

11. John Milner

12. John Milner

13. Ron Swoboda

14. 79

15. Rusty Staub—76 RBIs

16. Felix Millan—.290

17. Tommie Agee

18. Lee Mazzilli

19. Hubie Brooks hit safely in 24 straight games.

20. Cleon Jones—.340

21. Mookie Wilson

22. Tommie Agee

23. Rusty Staub and Gary Carter each drove in 105 runs.

At the Plate and on the Bases—Answers

24. John Stearns—25

25. Kranepool—225; Kiner—216

26. 70

27. Steve Henderson

28. Tommie Agee

29. Felix Millan

30. Seven

31. Mike Vail

32. Len Randle

33. Art Shamsky

34. Joel Youngblood

35. Hubie Brooks

36. Lee Mazzilli

37. Felix Millan

38. Frank Thomas

39. Rod Kanehl

40. Mike Howard

At the Plate and on the Bases—Answers

41. Hubie Brooks

42. Dick Stuart

43. Felix Millan

44. Joe Pignatano

45. .323

46. Ed Kranepool (56 hits; 144 times at bat)

47. Len Randle stole 33 bases in 1977, a club record.

48. Cleon Jones

49. Lee Mazzilli

50. Ken Boswell had 51 official at-bats as a pinch-hitter in 1973.

51. Bruce Boisclair; 12 hits in 21 times at bat for a .571 average

52. Cleon Jones

53. Joe Torre (1975)

54. Dave Schneck

55. Felix Millan

56. Snider—14; Hodges—9

At the Plate and on the Bases—Answers

57. Duke Snider

58. Jerry Grote

59. Hodges hit 14 grand-slammers.

60. Darryl Strawberry hit 26 homers as a Mets rookie in 1983.

61. Frank Thomas

62. Bob Johnson

63. Chris Cannizzaro

64. Ed Charles

65. Ken Boswell

66. Kevin Collins

67. Bob Heise

68. Bud Harrelson

69. Richie Ashburn and Elio Chacon stole 12 bases each.

70. Chuck Hiller

71. Ron Swoboda (August 15, 1965)

72. Rusty Staub

At the Plate and on the Bases—Answers

73. Rusty Staub

74. Mike Vail hit in 23 straight games.

75. Randy Tate

76. Five times, including once in the World Series

77. 14

78. Jim Hickman

79. Ashburn's 2,500th hit; Snider's 2,000th hit and 400th homer

80. A personal record for home runs in one season—five. He finished the season (his last) with seven.

81. Frank Thomas

82. Marv Throneberry

83. Frank Thomas

84. Tim Harkness

85. Dick Smith

86. Rusty Staub

87. Joe Christopher

At the Plate and on the Bases—Answers

88. Warren Spahn

89. Ron Swoboda

90. Ron Hunt. On May 14, 1966, Hunt singled three times and walked at Shea. On the following day, Hunt again smacked three singles and reached base on a fielder's choice before striking out. The next weekend, in San Francisco, Hunt homered, singled twice, was hit by a pitch and walked. In the next game, Hunt hit three more singles and was hit by a pitch. Totals: one home run, 11 singles, three bases on balls, twice hit by a pitch, one fielder's choice and one strike-out in 19 trips to the plate.

91. Art Shamsky hit three homers in 4 innings as a Red in 1966.

92. Steve Henderson

93. Boyer's 2,000th hit came on May 10, 1967.

94. Jim Hickman ruined no-hitters against the Dodgers and Braves; Cleon Jones, against the Braves and Reds; Ron Swoboda, against the Braves and Dogers; and John Stearns, against the Expos and Cardinals.

95. Weis batted .455, which included four singles, four walks and a game-tying

At the Plate and on the Bases—Answers

homer in the 7th inning of the final game.

96. Cleon Jones made four singles and two doubles and walked four times in one afternoon in a doubleheader against the Astros.

97. Jerry Grote made eight straight singles (first seven against St. Louis).

98. Leroy Stanton

99. John Milner

100. Ron Swoboda

101. Ken Boswell

102. Jones socked his 1,000th hit on August 2 and Millan his 1,000th on August 3, 1973.

103. Cleon Jones

104. Torre hit in 16 straight games for the Mets.

105. Dave Kingman

106. Bud Harrelson

107. Richie Hebner

108. Elliott Maddox

At the Plate and on the Bases—Answers

109. John Stearns

110. Steve Henderson

111. Lee Mazzilli

112. Eighth

113. Despite three home runs by Kingman (then with the Cubs), the Mets won the game, 6-4.

114. Len Randle and Lee Mazzilli

115. Willie Mays and George Foster

116. Mookie Wilson

117. Dave Kingman batted .204 while leading the league in home runs with 37.

118. Mike Jorgensen

119. Mike Fitzgerald

120. Bob Bailor

121. George Foster

122. John Stearns

123. Don Drysdale

At the Plate and on the Bases—Answers

124. Carter was hit by a pitch.

125. Carter's 10th-inning home run beat the Cardinals 6-5. In his third Mets game, Carter homered for the only run of the game. In his fifth game as a Met, Carter also hit a game-winning homer.

126. Wally Backman

127. The Pittsburgh Pirates

128. Danny Heep

129. George Foster

130. Danny Heep

131. Darryl Strawberry

132. Keith Hernandez

133. Darryl Strawberry and Gary Carter

134. Rafael Santana

135. Darryl Strawberry

136. Ray Knight

137. Dave Magadan

138. John Gibbons and Stanley Jefferson

At the Plate and on the Bases—Answers

139. Wally Backman

140. Gary Carter

141. Len Dykstra batted .304.

142. .189

143. Jesse Orosco

144. Ray Knight had nine hits; Gary Carter had nine RBIs.

Photographs

The New York Mets

1. In 1983 Darryl Strawberry became one of four Mets to receive what honor?

65

Photographs—Questions

The New York Mets

2. Did Jerry Koosman set, tie or come up short of the National League record for shutouts in a rookie year?

Photographs—Questions

Baseball Hall of Fame

3. Donn Clendenon once drove in 97 runs on only 114 hits. What year did he do this?

Photographs—Questions

The New York Mets

4. How many starts did Jon Matlack get in the 1973 World Series?

Photographs—Questions

5. Who is this player and what is he doing?

Photographs—Questions

The New York Mets

6. What Yogi Berra comment rang particularly true in Game 6 of the 1986 World Series?

70

Photographs—Questions

The New York Mets

7. In 1975 Felix Millan set the Mets single-season record for hits. How many did he have?

Photographs—Questions

The New York Mets

8. Name this pitcher, who shut the Red Sox down in Game 7 of the 1986 World Series.

Photographs—Questions

9. On May 21, 1972, Willie Mays's blast enabled the Mets to win their 11th straight game. Who are the Mets greeting Mays?

Photographs—Questions

Baseball Hall of Fame

10. How many years was Casey Stengel a manager?

Photographs—Questions

Baseball Hall of Fame

11. What year did Cleon Jones set the Mets one-season batting average high of .340?

Photographs—Questions

The New York Mets

12.   Name this current Mets pitcher.

76

Photographs—Questions

The New York Mets

13. From 1974 through 1978 what was Ed Kranepool's specialty?

Photographs—Questions

Baseball Hall of Fame

14. In 1970 Jerry Grote set what record?

Photographs—Questions

Baseball Hall of Fame

15. What year did Tommie Agee set the Mets single-season mark for runs scored (107), total bases (298) and extra-base hits (61)?

Photographs—Questions

Baseball Hall of Fame

16. Who are these former Brooklyn Dodgers and what year were they Mets teammates?

Photographs—Questions

Baseball Hall of Fame

17. How many years did the Mets play in the Polo Grounds?

81

Photographs—Questions

Baseball Hall of Fame

18.   Name this player.

Photographs—Questions

Baseball Hall of Fame

19. Ron Hunt was the first Met to start in what game?

83

Photographs—Questions

The New York Mets

20. How many errors did Bud Harrelson make in the 1969 World Series?

Photographs—Questions

21. Name this Mets star.

Baseball Hall of Fame

85

Photographs—Questions

The New York Mets

22. Rusty Staub has been the only player in baseball history to accomplish what for four different teams?

Photographs—Questions

Baseball Hall of Fame

23. Who is this man and what position did he play?

87

Photographs—Questions

The New York Mets

24. What year did Mets attendance surpass that of all previous New York teams?

Photographs—Questions

Baseball Hall of Fame

25. What year did John Milner join the team?

Photographs—Questions

26. How many times did Dave Kingman play for the Mets?

Photographs—Questions

The New York Mets

27. Name this Mets player, traded at different points for both Dave Kingman and Tom Seaver.

Photographs—Questions

The New York Mets

28.   In 1983 Jesse Orosco won both games of a doubleheader against what team?

Photographs—Questions

The New York Mets

29. What was Dwight Gooden's ERA and won-loss record in 1985?

Photographs—Questions

The New York Mets

30. How many game-winning homers did Gary Carter have in his first five games as a Met?

Photographs—Questions

The New York Mets

31. Who does Keith Hernandez consult when his hitting isn't up to snuff?

Photographs—Questions

The New York Mets

32. In what categories does Mookie Wilson lead the Mets, all-time?

Photographs—Questions

The New York Mets

33. Name this Mets star.

97

Photographs—Questions

The New York Mets

34. George Foster hit over 50 homers with what other major league club?

Photographs—Questions

The New York Mets

35. Name this current Mets standout.

Photographs—Questions

The New York Mets

36. This player pitched without a loss for seven weeks during the 1985 season. Who is he?

Answers

1. Rookie of the Year

2. Koosman tied the record.

3. 1970

4. Three

5. Tug McGraw celebrates the Mets' National League East title in 1973.

6. "It's not over till it's over."

7. 191

8. Sid Fernandez

Photographs—Answers

9. Jim Beauchamp (left) and Bud Harrelson

10. 25

11. 1969

12. Ron Darling

13. Pinch-hitting

14. Consecutive putouts (ten)

15. 1970

16. Gil Hodges and Duke Snider—1963

17. Two

18. Al Jackson

19. The All-Star Game

20. None—he handled 64 chances perfectly.

21. Marv Throneberry

22. Get 500 hits or more

23. Ron Swoboda; right field

24. 1970

25. 1972

Photographs—Answers

26. Twice

27. Steve Henderson

28. The Pittsburgh Pirates

29. 1.53; 24-4

30. Three

31. His brother and his father

32. Base-stealing and triples

33. Joe Torre

34. The Cincinnati Reds

35. Wally Backman

36. Ed Lynch

On the Mound

1. In 1970 Tom Seaver tied a major league record by striking out 19 batters in a game. What other record did he set that day?

2. As a Met, Tom Seaver won three Cy Young awards. Name the years.

3. Who was the first Mets pitcher to win 19 games in one season?

4. Name three former Cy Young Award winners who were with the Mets in 1981.

5. How many shutouts did Jerry Koosman pitch in his rookie year?

On the Mound—Questions

6. When Tom Seaver set the one-season National League record for strikeouts by a right-handed pitcher, how many did he fan?

7. What relief pitcher led the club in saves in the 1969 championship season?

8. Name the relief ace who led the team in saves four years in a row.

9. Who led National League left-handers in saves in 1972?

10. In which pitching category has Seaver most frequently led the National League?

11. Name the two Mets pitchers who combined for a 5-0 shutout over the Baltimore Orioles in the 1969 World Series.

12. Which two Mets pitchers combined for a 2-0 shutout over the Oakland A's in the 1973 World Series?

13. Who was the starting pitcher in three World Series games in 1973?

14. Who was the only pitcher to win a game in the first two Mets World Series appearances (1969 and 1973)?

15. Which Mets hurler lost 18 games in a row in 1963?

On the Mound—Questions

16. Who saved 22 games for the Mets in 1980?

17. Who pitched two two-hitters for the Mets in 1979?

18. Who was a 20-game winner and 20-game loser for the Mets?

19. Who led the National League in earned run average in 1978?

20. Which Mets pitcher was Rookie of the Year with the Cincinnati Reds?

21. Which 1980 Mets hurlers pitched for Montreal in 1981?

22. What was Tom Seaver's best earned run average?

23. Who was the ace of the Mets bullpen in 1976?

24. How many times did Seaver strike out 200 or more batters in a season?

25. Which Mets pitcher lost the most games in one season?

26. In which years did the Mets have two 20-game losers?

On the Mound—Questions

27. What was Tom Seaver's top victory total?

28. How many seasons did Nino Espinosa pitch for the Mets?

29. In 1969 who broke up Tom Seaver's perfect game bid with one out in the 9th inning?

30. Which 1981 Mets pitcher was once a 20-game loser and then a 20-game winner for another club?

31. Which Mets pitching star gave up Roberto Clemente's 3,000 hit?

32. Who pitched five no-hitters after leaving the Mets?

33. Who pitched all 15 innings for the Mets in a game against the Phillies?

34. Who was the only Mets pitcher with a winning record in 1962?

35. Which Mets pitcher tied a record by striking out the first six batters in a game?

36. Which Mets pitcher won one game in 1962, then came back to New York 12 years later to win two more for the Mets?

37. Who had five four-hit games in 1980?

On the Mound—Questions

38. Which Mets pitcher was once a 29-year-old American League rookie?

39. Who won 12 out of 15 decisions for the 1973 Mets?

40. Who pitched six shutouts for the 1969 Mets?

41. How many consecutive years did Tom Seaver strike out over 200 batters?

42. Who set a Mets record by pitching in 62 games in 1964?

43. Who set a Mets record by pitching in 63 games in 1977?

44. Which Mets pitcher was a bonus baby with the Kansas City A's in 1964—as a third baseman?

45. Which Mets pitcher once won three games in one World Series while pitching in the American League?

46. Identify the two-season Mets pitcher who appeared in over 400 games in relief (career) but started only one game.

47. Which four Mets won Cy Young Awards with their former clubs?

On the Mound—Questions

48. Name the Met who pitched no-hit ball against Montreal for 7⅓ innings and lost the game?

49. Who was Tom Seaver's 2,000th strikeout victim?

50. Which Met was one strike away from a no-hitter?

51. What was unusual about Tom Seaver winning the Rookie of the Year award?

52. Which team did Seaver originally sign with?

53. Which rookie led the pitching staff in appearances in 1975?

54. Who held the Mets record for lifetime wins before Tom Seaver broke it in 1969?

55. Lou Brock called him "toughest catcher to steal against." Name him.

56. Who had an 0-4 record, then came back to win six straight in 1968?

57. Who was the first Mets pitcher to defeat Sandy Koufax?

58. Out of his nine wins in 1968, this pitcher won six in a row. Name him.

On the Mound—Questions

59. The Mets tied a record in 1967 by using quite a few pitchers. Was it: a)16, b)19, c)22 or d)27?

60. Which Mets pitcher lost 46 games in two seasons?

61. Which Mets pitcher had a 17-1 record at Arizona State?

62. Who was the only pitcher to toss a no-hitter in his first start after being traded?

63. Which left-hander pitched ten career shutouts for the Mets prior to 1969?

64. Which pitcher had no runs scored for him in his first four major league starts?

65. This Mets rookie shut out the Reds with four hits in his first start. He never won another major league game. Name him.

66. In the first five years of the Mets, two pitchers tossed one-hitters. Name the hurlers.

67. Who wore a Superman t-shirt under his uniform in the 1973 World Series?

68. Who pitched eight consecutive complete games in 1976?

69. Which Mets pitcher retired with a perfect 2-0 record?

On the Mound—Questions

70. How did Roger Craig's 18-game losing streak come to an end?

71. Who was the first National League pitcher in 52 years to lose 16 straight games?

72. Which of the following pitched all of the Mets' shutouts in 1962: Al Jackson, Roger Craig or Jay Hook?

73. Who was the first right-hander to pitch a shutout for the Mets?

74. Identify the Mets pitcher whose jaw was broken by Gates Brown's line drive?

75. Who tied a major league record by striking out four pinch-hitters in one game?

76. Who pitched a one-hitter against the Mets six months after being sold by them?

77. Who set a Mets record in 1965 by striking out 13 batters while pitching a 10-inning shutout over the Braves?

78. Who pitched the second one-hitter in Mets history?

79. Who pitched a one-hitter and was relieved in his next start with a two-hitter in progress?

On the Mound—Questions

80. Who was the first Mets starting pitcher to win four games in a row?

81. Who was the first Mets pitcher to win six straight games: Al Jackson, Jerry Koosman, Tom Seaver or Dick Selma?

82. Did Tom Seaver ever pitch in both ends of a doubleheader?

83. Other than Tug McGraw, who was the only Mets pitcher to beat Sandy Koufax?

84. In 1969 Mets pitchers accomplished an amazing feat. This achievement took place over a total of 221 innings and it involved 22 full games. What did they do?

85. Excluding Don Buford's double and home run in the opening game of the 1969 World Series, how many extra-base hits did Mets pitchers allow going into the final game?

86. Whose lifetime record includes seven innings pitched in World Series competition (not all with the Mets), with no hits given up?

87. From August 6, 1969, to May 11, 1970, how many times did Tom Seaver defeat National League opponents without a loss?

On the Mound—Questions

88. Which three Mets pitched one-hitters in 1970?

89. Who was the winning pitcher in the Mets first victory over Juan Marichal?

90. Whose first career victory came against Juan Marichal?

91. Which hurler defeated the Dodgers eight times in a row?

92. Who was Tom Seaver's 1,000th strikeout victim?

93. How many times did Tom Seaver beat the Padres before they beat him once?

94. Who beat the Phillies 11 times in a row?

95. Who lost 19 games in a row: Roger Craig or Craig Anderson?

96. Which team did Seaver, Matlack and Swan win their first games against?

97. How many shutouts did Tug McGraw pitch as a Met?

98. Between 1969 and 1972, who made 124 relief appearances for the Mets, with only one game as a starter?

On the Mound—Questions

99. What did the following players have in common: Jim Qualls, Mike Compton, Vic Davalillo, Leron Lee, Joe Wallis and Steve Ontiveros?

100. Did Tom Seaver, Jerry Koosman and Jon Matlack ever appear in the same game?

101. In 1976, when Jerry Koosman won his 20th game, who was the losing pitcher? Hint: he later became a Met.

102. Including 1983, how many times did Tom Seaver pitch the opening game of the season as a New York Met?

103. When Seaver faced the Mets for the first time after being traded, who was the pitching opponent and what was the outcome?

104. As a Met, how many times did Seaver have a no-hitter going into the 9th inning?

105. Who gave up all the runs scored by the American League in the 1975 and 1976 All-Star Games?

106. Who gave up the record-tying and record-breaking hits as Pete Rose broke Tommy Holmes's National League hitting-streak record?

On the Mound—Questions

107. Before Tom Seaver returned to the Mets in 1983, who pitched in more games for the club: Seaver or Jerry Koosman?

108. Prior to 1983, what was Tom Seaver's won-lost record in opening games?

109. Before coming to the Mets, who once pitched 68 consecutive innings without allowing a walk?

110. Which rookie pitcher lost a 1-0 game on a balk?

111. In July 1983 which Mets pitcher won both games of a doubleheader?

112. Which Mets pitcher won four games in one week?

113. In 1984 who was the first Met left-hander to start and win a game in almost two years?

114. Who got the only base hit in Dwight Gooden's first one-hitter?

115. When Dwight Gooden struck out 16 batters for the second straight game, whose National League record of 31 strikeouts in two games was broken?

116. In 1985, who won the John J. Murphy Award as the best rookie in spring training?

On the Mound—Questions

117. After leadoff batter Johnny Ray singled in the first inning, which two Mets combined to no-hit the Pirates?

118. In addition to Dwight Gooden, which Met pitcher went seven weeks without a loss in 1985: Ron Darling, Sid Fernandez or Ed Lynch?

119. In 1985, exactly how old was Dwight Gooden when he won his 20th game of the season?

120. How many consecutive games did Gooden win in 1985?

121. From August 12, 1984, to the end of the 1985 season, what was Dwight Gooden's won-lost record?

122. Name the pitcher who became the first Met to win seven games and lose none at the start of a season?

123. Who became the first pitcher in major league history to strike out 200 or more batters in his first three seasons?

124. Who won a total of 20 games for the Mets in 1985 and 1986, yet never won a game before June 12th?

125. Which Mets hurlers struck out 200 or more batters in 1986?

On the Mound—Questions

126. Who was the big winner on the 1986 pitching staff?

Answers

1. Seaver struck out ten men in a row—the last ten batters he faced.

2. 1969, 1973 and 1975

3. Jerry Koosman

4. Randy Jones, Mike Marshall and Coach Bob Gibson

5. Seven

6. 283 in 1970; 289 in 1971

7. Ron Taylor—13

On the Mound—Answers

8. Ron Taylor—1967 through 1970

9. Tug McGraw—27

10. Strikeouts—five times

11. Gary Gentry and Nolan Ryan

12. Jerry Koosman and Tug McGraw

13. Jon Matlack

14. Jerry Koosman

15. Roger Craig

16. Neil Allen

17. Craig Swan

18. Jerry Koosman

19. Craig Swan

20. Pat Zachry

21. Ray Burris and Jeff Reardon

22. 1.76 in 1971

23. Skip Lockwood had 10 wins and 19 saves.

On the Mound—Answers

24. Ten

25. Roger Craig (1962) and Jack Fisher (1965) each lost 24.

26. 1962 (Craig and Jackson) and 1965 (Fisher and Jackson)

27. 25 wins in 1969

28. Five

29. Rookie Jim Qualls

30. Randy Jones

31. Jon Matlack

32. Nolan Ryan

33. Al Jackson

34. Ken McKenzie won five and lost four.

35. Pete Falcone

36. Bob Miller

37. Frank Taveras

38. Dyar Miller

39. George Stone

On the Mound—Answers

40. Jerry Koosman

41. Nine

42. Bill Wakefield

43. Skip Lockwood

44. Skip Lockwood

45. Mickey Lolich

46. Ken Sanders

47. Warren Spahn, Dean Chance, Mike Marshall and Randy Jones

48. Randy Tate

49. Dan Driessen

50. Tom Seaver

51. It was the first time a National League player on a last-place team won.

52. The Braves

53. Rick Baldwin—54

54. Al Jackson

55. Jerry Grote

On the Mound—Answers

56. Cal Koonce

57. Tug McGraw (August 26, 1965)

58. Dick Selma

59. 27

60. Roger Craig

61. Gary Gentry

62. Don Cardwell for Cubs (against Cardinals)

63. Al Jackson

64. Jim McAndrew

65. Dick Rusteck (1966)

66. Al Jackson (June 22, 1962) and Jack Hamilton (May 4, 1966)

67. Bud Harrelson

68. Jerry Koosman

69. Jim Bethke

70. On a 3-2 count, Jim Hickman hit a two-out, 9th-inning, bases-loaded homer to beat the Cubs 7-3.

On the Mound—Answers

71. Craig Anderson

72. Al Jackson pitched all four Mets shutouts in 1962.

73. Carl Willey, 2-0 over the Cubs

74. Carl Willey (1964)

75. Galen Cisco

76. Gerry Arrigo

77. Dick Selma

78. Jack Hamilton (May 4, 1966)

79. Jack Hamilton

80. Bob Shaw

81. Dick Selma

82. Yes. On August 17, 1967, Seaver pitched the first two innings of the opener. He returned to the mound to relieve in the second game.

83. Bob Friend

84. Mets pitchers allowed no home runs in 22 consecutive games during 1969.

On the Mound—Answers

85. Excluding Don Buford's double and home run in Game 1, Mets pitchers allowed no doubles, triples or homers going into the final game.

86. Ron Taylor pitched in World Series games with the Cardinals in 1964 and with the Mets in 1969. He pitched 7 innings all told and allowed no hits.

87. Seaver won his last ten games in 1969. Then he defeated the Braves in the playoffs. From the start of the 1970 season, Tom won his first six games. Total: 17 wins in a row.

88. Nolan Ryan, Gary Gentry and Tom Seaver

89. Jack Fisher won in relief, 8-7, after Marichal had beaten the Mets 19 times in a row. Previously Jack had ended Bob Friend's 12-game streak over the Mets. Fisher was also the first Mets hurler to beat Larry Jackson who had an 18-game win streak over the Mets.

90. Charlie Williams (1971)

91. Tom Seaver

92. Willie Montanez

On the Mound—Answers

93. Seaver won ten games in a row from the Padres before they beat him for the first time in May 1972.

94. Tom Seaver

95. Craig Anderson dropped the last 19 games of his career.

96. The Chicago Cubs

97. McGraw pitched his only shutout on September 1, 1974.

98. Danny Frisella

99. Each man ruined a no-hit bid by Tom Seaver.

    Seaver one-hitters: *Spoilers*   *Team*
    July 9, 1969   Jim Qualls   Cubs
    May 15, 1970   Mike Compton   Phillies
    Sept. 26, 1971   Vic Davalillo   Pirates
    July 4, 1972   Leron Lee   Padres
    Sept. 24, 1975*   Joe Wallis   Cubs
    April 17, 1977   Steve Ontiveros   Cubs

    *In the 1975 game, Seaver gave up two more hits in the 10th inning. He was then taken out of the game. The Mets lost 1-0 in the 11th inning (Lockwood lost).

100. Yes, in 1976. Matlack started; Koosman and Seaver pitched in relief.

101. Pete Falcone

On the Mound—Answers

102. Seaver started the season for the Mets 11 times.

103. Jerry Koosman pitched against the Reds. Seaver beat the Mets 5-1.

104. Tom Seaver had three no-hit games going into the 9th inning.

105. Tom Seaver

106. Pat Zachry gave up the hit that Rose needed to tie Holmes's record. On the next day (July 25, 1978), Craig Swan gave up the hit that enabled Rose to break the record.

107. Koosman pitched in 376 Met games; Seaver pitched in 367.

108. Seaver won six openers; lost none.

109. Randy Jones

110. Rick Ownbey

111. Jesse Orosco

112. Jesse Orosco

113. Sid Fernandez

114. Keith Moreland

On the Mound—Answers

115. Sandy Koufax

116. Roger McDowell

117. Ron Darling (7) and Jesse Orosco (2)

118. Ed Lynch

119. 20 years, 9 months and 9 days old.

120. 14

121. Believe it or not, Gooden won 32 and lost 5.

122. Roger McDowell

123. Dwight Gooden

124. Rick Aguilera

125. Dwight Gooden and Sid Fernandez each struck out exactly 200.

126. Bob Ojeda won 18 games.

On the Field

1. What Mets player led the league in putouts at his position in 1970 and 1971?

2. Which Met handled 849 chances in 1971 and made only two errors?

3. How many years did Ed Kranepool play for the Mets?

4. What catcher took part in a league-leading twelve double plays in 1972?

5. Which Met led the league in assists and double plays and narrowly missed 100 RBIs in his first year with the team?

On the Field—Questions

6. Which four Mets have won Gold Glove awards?

7. Which Met tied a one-season major league record for shortstops of 54 straight errorless games?

8. Which infielder took part in six double plays in one game against the Mets? Hint: he later became a Met.

9. Which Mets shortstop participated in triple plays in 1964 and 1965?

10. He played over 700 games at third base for the Mets from 1969 through the mid-seventies. Name him.

11. Who was the Mets' first first baseman?

12. The Mets' opening-day lineup for the first six years (1962-1967) featured a different first baseman each year. Name them.

13. The Mets' opening-day lineup for the first seven years (1962-1968) featured a different second baseman each year. Name them.

14. The Mets' opening-day lineup for the first five years featured a different third baseman each year. Name them.

On the Field—Questions

15. The Mets' opening-day lineup for the first five years featured a different catcher each year. Name them.

16. Who was the Brooklyn-born third baseman who appeared in over 100 games for the 1971 Mets?

17. In 1966 who were the two Mets infielders known as "Iron Hands" and "Dr. Strangeglove"?

18. Which original Met was great at catching the baseball barehanded?

19 In 1970 who set the major league record for consecutive errorless games by a second baseman?

20. Who caught for the first and only time when Jerry Grote was thrown out of a game?

21. Who played six positions for the 1986 Mets?

22. When Ray Knight was ejected with several others after a fight with Eric Davis, who replaced him at third base?

23. Which Mets outfielder led the National League in assists in 1974 and 1975?

On the Field—Questions

24. Which Mets outfielder was credited with 18 assists in 1979?

25. Who made two spectacular catches in the same game in the World Series of 1969?

26. Whose diving catch robbed Brooks Robinson of a sure triple in the 1969 World Series?

27. Name the Mets' opening-day rightfielders from 1962 to 1966.

28. Which Mets player won a Gold Glove in both leagues?

29. Which Mets outfielders collided on Terry Pendleton's inside-the-park grand slam homer?

Answers

1. Jerry Grote

2. Ed Kranepool—998

3. 18

4. Duffy Dyer

5. Willie Montanez

6. Tommie Agee, Bud Harrelson, Doug Flynn and Keith Hernandez

7. Bud Harrelson

8. Felix Millan

On the Field—Answers

9. Roy McMillan

10. Wayne Garrett

11. Gil Hodges

12. 1962—Gil Hodges; 1963—Tim Harkness; 1964—Dick Smith; 1965—Ed Kranepool; 1966—Dick Stuart; and 1967—Ron Swoboda

13. 1962—Charlie Neal; 1963—Larry Burright; 1964—Amado Samuel; 1965—Bobby Klaus; 1966—Ron Hunt; 1967—Jerry Buckek; and 1968—Ken Boswell

14. 1962—Don Zimmer; 1963—Charlie Neal; 1964—Ron Hunt; 1965—Charley Smith; and 1966—Ken Boyer

15. 1962—Hobie Landrith; 1963—Choo Choo Coleman; 1964—Hawk Taylor; 1965—Chris Cannizzaro; and 1966—Jerry Grote

16. Bob Aspromonte

17. Chuck Hiller and Dick Stuart

18. Frank Thomas

19. Ken Boswell (85 games)

On the Field—Answers

20. Tommy Reynolds

21. Kevin Mitchell

22. Gary Carter came in to play third base for the first time in eleven years.

23. Rusty Staub threw out 19 runners in 1974 and 15 in 1975.

24. Joel Youngblood

25. Tommie Agee

26. Ron Swoboda

27. 1962—Gus Bell; 1963—Ed Kranepool; 1964—Joe Christopher; 1965—Johnny Lewis; and 1966—Cleon Jones

28. Tommie Agee

29. Terry Blocker and Danny Heep

Trades

1. This Met played in over 2,000 games with other clubs. In his only season with the Mets he socked nearly one-fourth of his lifetime home runs. Name him.

2. Which players hit four home runs in one game prior to joining the Mets?

3. Whom did the Mets receive when they traded Wayne Garrett and Del Unser?

4. On April 5, 1972, whom did the Mets give up in order to get Rusty Staub?

5. In 1979, when the Mets traded Tim Foli for the second time, whom did they acquire?

Trades—Questions

6. Who were the other players involved in the first Seaver trade?

7. Which Mets pitcher was traded for Ellis Valentine?

8. What team did John Stearns play for before becoming a Met?

9. Name the team Jerry Grote played for prior to becoming a Met.

10. Who played for the Padres, Cubs, Cardinals and Tigers before becoming a Met?

11. Who pitched for the Orioles, Angels and Blue Jays before hurling for the Mets?

12. Who played for the Mets, then the Expos, A's and Rangers, before returning to the Mets?

13. Name the two-time National League batting champions that became Mets.

14. Who played for the A's, Rangers and White Sox before coming to the Mets?

15. Which Met played for the Tigers, Senators, Rangers, Yankees and Orioles before coming to Shea?

16. Which third baseman did the Mets obtain in exchange for Nolan Ryan?

Trades—Questions

17. Whom did the Mets trade for Willie Mays?

18. Which player went to Washington in November 1967 in exchange for Gil Hodges?

19. Which six Mets won Most Valuable Player awards with their former clubs?

20. What team did Cleon Jones finish his playing career with?

21. Which right-handed pitcher beat the Mets 12 times in a row? Hint: later he became a Met.

22. Who caught for the Reds, Cubs, Cards, Giants and Mets?

23. Which player was purchased from Cleveland for a player to be named later, and turned out to be traded for himself?

24. In December 1967, whom did the Mets give up to get Tommie Agee and Al Weis?

25. Which American League teams did Tommie Agee play for?

26. Who played nine years with the White Sox before coming to the Mets?

27. When Ken Boyer was traded to the White Sox, whom did the Mets obtain?

Trades—Questions

28. The first two players in National League history to hit bases-loaded home runs in the World Series later became Mets. Who were they?

29. Which team did Rusty Staub play for prior to becoming a Met?

30. This pitcher started his career as a Met. He later pitched for the Cubs, Indians, Yanks, A's and Brewers. His best season was 1972 (with the Yankees). Name him.

31. Name the catcher who caught for six American League teams before becoming a Met.

32. Name the two World-Series-winning managers who were Mets players at one time.

33. Who pitched for the Mets in 1965 and managed the Cardinals in 1978?

34. Who played for the Mets in 1962 and managed the Cubs in 1974?

35. Who was the Brooklyn-born catcher who played for the Dodgers, Giants and Mets?

36. Who played for the Mets in 1963 and managed California in 1976?

Trades—Questions

37. Which Mets third baseman was once traded for Roger Maris?

38. Name the players (six) involved in the Tug McGraw trade.

39. Which three one-time Mets homered in their first World Series at-bat?

40. When Jerry Grote's right wrist was broken by a pitched ball, whom did the Mets purchase from Kansas City to back up catcher Duffy Dyer?

41. Whom did the Mets give up to get Felix Millan and George Stone?

42. What did Tommy Davis and Bob Miller have in common?

43. Who was the catcher who asked to be sent back to the minors (in order to play more often)?

44. Who was traded by the Mets and came back two days later to beat them with an 11th-inning homer?

45. Who was once traded for Tom Seaver and also traded for Dave Kingman?

46. Name the pitcher who was traded for two MVPs.

Trades—Questions

47. Who tied a major league record by playing for four teams in one year (and in all four divisions, yet)?

48. Which two Mets on the 1982 club were teammates on the 1971 Giants?

49. Name six Mets on the 1979-1980 club that played on the Expos in 1982.

50. Who spent eight years in the National League and then eight years in the American League before becoming a Met in 1983?

51. Who played for the Mets from 1973 to 1984?

Answers

1. Richie Ashburn. In 1962 Ashburn hit seven home runs for the Mets. His lifetime total was 29.

2. Gil Hodges—Brooklyn Dodgers (1950) and Willie Mays—San Francisco Giants (1961)

3. Pepe Mangual and Jim Dwyer

4. Ken Singleton, Tim Foli and Mike Jorgensen

5. Frank Taveras

6. Doug Flynn, Steve Henderson, Dan Norman and Pat Zachry

Trades—Answers

7. Jeff Reardon

8. The Philadelphia Phillies

9. The Houston Colts

10. Jerry Morales

11. Dyar Miller

12. Mike Jorgensen

13. Richie Ashburn (1955 and 1958) and Tommy Davis (1962 and 1963)

14. Claudell Washington

15. Elliott Maddox

16. Jim Fregosi

17. Pitcher Charlie Williams

18. Pitcher Bill Denehy

19. Yogi Berra, Willie Mays, Ken Boyer, Joe Torre, George Foster and Keith Hernandez

20. Chicago White Sox

21. Bob Friend

Trades—Answers

22. Hobie Landrith

23. Harry Chiti

24. Tommy Davis, Jack Fisher, Billy Wynne and a minor league catcher, Buddy Booker

25. The Cleveland Indians and the Chicago White Sox

26. J.C. Martin

27. J.C. Martin

28. Chuck Hiller and Ken Boyer

29. The Montreal Expos

30. Rob Gardner

31. Joe Ginsberg

32. Gil Hodges and Dallas Green

33. Gary Kroll (managed three Cardinals games)

34. Jim Marshall

35. Joe Pignatano

36. Norm Sherry

Trades—Answers

37. Charley Smith

38. McGraw and outfielders Don Hahn and Dave Schneck went to the Phillies in exchange for catcher John Stearns, outfielder Del Unser and pitcher Mac Scarce.

39. Mickey Lolich (Detroit), Amos Otis (Kansas City) and Jim Dwyer (Baltimore)

40. Jerry May

41. Gary Gentry and Danny Frisella

42. Both played for ten major league teams.

43. John Stearns

44. Del Unser

45. Steve Henderson

46. Pitcher Ray Sadecki was involved in separate trades for MVPs Orlando Cepeda and Joe Torre.

47. Dave Kingman (1977)

48. George Foster and Dave Kingman

49. Ray Burris, Doug Flynn, Dan Norman, Jeff Reardon, Frank Taveras and Joel Youngblood

Trades—Answers

50. Mike Torrez

51. Ron Hodges

Managers and Coaches

1. When did Casey Stengel enter the Baseball Hall of Fame?

2. What was Salty Parker's record as Mets manager?

3. Which manager served the Mets longest: Stengel, Hodges, Berra or Torre?

4. Who was called "The Old Professor"?

5. Name the manager who said: "It's not over 'til it's over."

6. When did Roy McMillan manage the Mets?

Managers and Coaches—Questions

7. Which Mets coach was known as "The Walking Man"?

8. Name the Mets manager who led the club to an 86-76 record in 1976.

9. What was Roy McMillan's record as Mets manager?

10. How many years did Casey Stengel play in the big leagues?

11. Which team did Gil Hodges manage before the Mets?

12. Prior to Dave Johnson, only one Mets manager had a lifetime winning record. Name the man.

13. This former first baseman-outfielder was a batting instructor for the Mets. He won a batting championship with a .355 average. Name the man.

14. Among Mets coaches in 1981 was a Harlem Globetrotter. Name him.

15. Which Mets general manager was once a Yankee pitching star?

16. Name the Mets coaches who wore uniform numbers 52, 53 and 54, working together for at least eight years?

Managers and Coaches—Questions

17. Which former Mets pitching coach once pitched 12 perfect innings in a game?

18. Which former Mets manager was at bat over 7,000 times in the minor leagues?

19. Which Mets coach is in the New York University Hall of Fame?

20. What did Solly Hemus, Rogers Hornsby, Red Kress, Cookie Lavagetto and Red Ruffing have in common?

21. How many games did Casey Stengel win as manager of the Mets?

22. Who was the first manager to lead the Mets out of last place?

23. Who managed the Mets between Wes Westrum and Gil Hodges?

24. During his playing days, how many times was Gil Hodges thrown out of a game?

25. Who managed the 1970 National League All-Star team?

26. Who managed the 1974 National League All-Star team?

27. Who was acting manager of the Mets for the final weekend of 1968?

Managers and Coaches—Questions

28. Before the start of the 1975 Old Timers Game at Shea Stadium, did Casey Stengel enter the field via sports car, Roman chariot or helicopter?

29. Name the four Mets managers who previously played for the Mets.

30. Who won more games as Mets manager: Yogi Berra or Joe Torre?

31. Which Mets managers wore the same uniform number?

32. Which Mets manager pitched for the New York Giants?

33. Which Mets manager hit the most home runs during his playing career: Yogi Berra, Gil Hodges or Frank Howard?

34. In Dave Johnson's first victory as Mets manager, who was the winning pitcher?

35. When Bobby Valentine left the Mets to become manager of the Texas Rangers, who replaced him as third-base coach?

ANSWERS

1. 1966

2. Parker won four games and lost seven as Mets manager in 1967.

3. Joe Torre

4. Casey Stengel

5. Yogi Berra

6. 1975

7. Eddie Yost

8. Joe Frazier

Managers and Coaches—Answers

9. 26 and 27

10. 14

11. The Washington Senators

12. Gil Hodges

13. Phil Cavaretta

14. Bob Gibson

15. Johnny Murphy

16. Joe Pignatano, Eddie Yost and Rube Walker

17. Harvey Haddix

18. Salty Parker

19. Eddie Yost

20. They were the original Mets coaches.

21. 175

22. Wes Westrum

23. Salty Parker

24. In 18 years as a player, Gil Hodges was never thrown out of a game by an umpire.

Managers and Coaches—Answers

25. Gil Hodges

26. Yogi Berra

27. Rube Walker

28. Roman chariot

29. Gil Hodges, Yogi Berra, Roy McMillan and Joe Torre were Mets managers who also played for the club.

30. Berra won 292 games; Torre won 286.

31. Wes Westrum and Joe Torre both wore number nine.

32. George Bamberger

33. Howard hit 382 homers; Hodges 370; Berra 358.

34. Ron Darling

35. Bud Harrelson

Miscellaneous

1. Who was known as "The Glider"?

2. Who said, "You gotta believe!"?

3. Who was born on the day Babe Ruth died?

4. What uniform number was worn by Ed Kranepool, Warren Spahn, Cleon Jones and Elliott Maddox?

5. What uniform number was worn by Jerry Koosman and Mark Bomback?

6. What uniform number was worn by Jerry

Miscellaneous—Questions

Grote, Claudell Washington and George Foster?

7. What uniform number was worn by Frank Taveras?

8. What is Rusty Staub's real first name?

9. Which players have had the same last name as Mets managers?

10. Which current Met hails from Hillsboro, Oregon?

11. Which Met was once a hot-dog vendor at Shea Stadium?

12. Who was a Mets rookie at 27 years of age?

13. How many seasons did Al Weis play for the Mets?

14. Name the pitcher known as Fat Jack.

15. Which three Mets first baseman were born on April Fool's Day?

16. Which batterymates share the same birthday?

17. Which Mets pitcher later became a doctor?

Miscellaneous—Questions

18. Name two Mets players whose sons became major league players.

19. Name two Mets whose fathers were major leaguers.

20. Who was called "The Hammer"?

21. How old was Ed Kranepool when he made his first major league hit?

22. Ed Kranepool, Tug McGraw, Tom Seaver and Rusty Staub were born in the same year. What year?

23. What was George Theodore's nickname?

24. Name the player known as "Choo Choo."

25. The Mets had four players named Taylor. Give their first names.

26. Which Mets pitchers were born on Christmas Day?

27. Which current player wears uniform number 1?

28. Who was known as "The Franchise"?

29. Who was last to wear uniform number 13?

Miscellaneous—Questions

30. Which Met hit a home run in the 1979 All-Star Game?

31. Which Mets president was a baseball executive for 56 years?

32. Which Mets catcher was a defensive halfback for Colorado?

33. What do pitchers Ed Lynch, Tom Hausman and Pat Zachry have in common?

34. Which Mets second baseman performed as a country and western singer?

35. Name the Mets pitcher who graduated from Yale.

36. What were the approximate odds for the Mets winning the pennant in 1969?

37. Name the baseball commissioner who picked Tom Seaver's name out of a hat and changed the course of baseball history.

38. Name the only Met chosen for the 1977 All-Star team.

39. Who was known as Cobra Joe?

40. Name the Mets pitcher whose father played for the Brooklyn Dodgers.

Miscellaneous—Questions

41. Which Mets outfielders were high school teammates?

42. Which Mets pitcher had a motorcycle fall on him when he was three years old?

43. In 1981 which two former Mets were the winning and losing pitchers in the fourth playoff game between Philadelphia and Montreal?

44. Which two unrelated Mets with the same last name played on the 1976 club?

45. Who was born on D-Day?

46. Who was called "The Blade"?

47. Identify the Met who was one of three brothers who played in a record total of over 5,000 major league games.

48. Who shared MVP honors with Bill Madlock in the 1975 All-Star Game?

49. Which third baseman was the Mets' first selection in the January 1970 free agent draft?

50. Who threw out the first ball to start the Mets-Reds playoff in 1973?

Miscellaneous—Questions

51. Which team did Mrs. Joan Payson root for before she became a Mets fan?

52. Which Mets star was American League Rookie of the Year in 1966?

53. Who passed up a pro football offer from the Cleveland Browns to sign with the Mets?

54. Name the four Texans on the 1969 roster.

55. Which future Met gave up Roger Maris's 60th home run in 1961?

56. Which future Met gave up Roger Maris's 61st home run in 1961?

57. What song did the organist play when Millan was the hero of the game?

58. Who was the first pitcher ever to face Gil Hodges?

59. Who was offered pro contracts with the Globetrotters, Knicks, Browns and Pirates and eventually became a Met?

60. What were the dimensions of the old Polo Grounds?

61. Name the pitcher who gave up Willie Mays's first home run.

Miscellaneous—Questions

62. Who knocked in both runs on the day the Brooklyn Dodgers won the World Series from the Yankees?

63. Which Mets pitcher was discovered by the son of a Shea Stadium usher?

64. Which Mets pitchers were teammates in high school?

65. Which team originally drafted Tom Seaver?

66. What is Tug McGraw's real first name?

67. Who wore uniform number 1 on the 1969 Mets roster?

68. Who became the Mets' president after George Weiss?

69. Name the two pitchers on the 1967 Mets roster with the same last name.

70. In 1962 who were the two Mets pitchers with the same name?

71. Who broke Hall of Famer Hank Greenberg's school record for homers at James Monroe High?

72. What is J.C. Martin's full name?

Miscellaneous—Questions

73. Who was the youngest of the 1969 Mets?

74. How many World Series games have the Mets played?

75. Who was known as "Rocky"?

76. Who pitched a no-hitter and a one-hitter against the Mets?

77. What do Sandy Alomar, Richie Ashburn and Roy McMillan have in common?

78. Who is the youngest of the Alou brothers?

79. How many games did Yogi Berra appear in as a Met?

80. Name seven Mets third basemen with brothers in the major leagues.

81. What did Mets pitchers Doc Medich, Vinegar Bend Mizell, Dean Chance and Ralph Terry have in common?

82. What team did the Mets defeat to end their 17-game losing streak?

83. Who was known as "Lucky"?

84. Why was the number 11 significant when the Dodgers defeated the Mets on May 31, 1962?

Miscellaneous—Questions

85. Why did Gene Woodling have to change his uniform number when he came to the Mets?

86. Only three players ever hit homers into the centerfield bleachers at the Polo Grounds. Name the two players who homered into the bleachers against the Mets on consecutive days.

87. Name the Met whose initials are M.E.T.

88. Who hit the three-run homer with two out in the bottom of the 9th inning to end the Mets' losing streak at 13 games?

89. Who got into a fight with Willie Mays?

90. Who wore uniform number 4 before Duke Snider?

91. Who was the winning pitcher in the game that ended the Mets' 17-game losing streak?

92. Who was the first to hit three homers in a game against the Mets?

93. What uniform number did Roger Craig wear as he ended his 18-game losing streak?

94. Which Mets pitcher surrendered Jerry Grote's first major league hit?

Miscellaneous—Questions

95. What was the standing between the Mets and Dodgers after the first fifty games were played between the two clubs?

96. In what year did Yogi Berra play for the Mets?

97. Who was known as "Clink"?

98. What uniform number was most popular with Mets catchers?

99. Why did switch-hitting pitcher Dick Selma decide not to switch-hit anymore?

100. Who twice belted three home runs in a game against the Mets: was it Hank Aaron, Willie Mays, Willie McCovey or Willie Stargell?

101. In which year did Cleon Jones first play for the Mets?

102. Which Cub hit three two-run homers in one game against the Mets, after hitting two homers in his previous game?

103. Trick Question: In 1969, which club scored 11 runs in one inning and another 10 runs three innings later against the Mets?

104. Which Mets player became a congressman?

Miscellaneous—Questions

105. Who did the Mets pass up when they drafted Steve Chilcott as their first free-agent pick in 1966?

106. In 1971 which hurler finally lost to the Mets after beating them nine times in a row?

107. Who were the first three sluggers to hit 40 homers against the Mets?

108. Who hit two homers in a game on his birthday?

109. Which Phillie had great success against Tom Seaver?

110. Who was known as "Crazy Horse"?

111. Who wore uniform number 24 before Willie Mays?

112. Who was the 18-year-old chosen first in the 1973 free-agent draft?

113. In 1972, when Steve Carlton won 27 and lost 10 for the last-place Phillies, how many times was he beaten by the Mets?

114. Who was the Atlanta batter that lined the baseball off Jon Matlack's head?

115. Going into the 1973 season, what pitcher

Miscellaneous—Questions

had a lifetime record of 25 wins and 4 losses against the Mets?

116. Which team was the victim of Willie Mays's final home run?

117. Name the pitcher who gave up Willie Mays's last homer.

118. Who was a teammate of Sandy Koufax, Willie Mays and Stan Musial?

119. When the Mets lost the World Series to the Oakland A's, what did the A's manager Dick Williams do?

120. Who pitched two one-hitters against the Mets, nine years apart?

121. Why were Mets games called off on July 13 and 14, 1977?

122. Which pitcher gave up Ted Williams's last home run?

123. Who was the catcher for the Brooklyn Dodgers on the day Bobby Thomson hit his pennant-winning homer: Roy Campanella, Gil Hodges, Rube Walker or Don Zimmer?

124. Which Dodgers record did Don Sutton tie when he beat the Mets on May 10, 1979?

Miscellaneous—Questions

125. Who pitched a 10-inning shutout over the Mets at the age of 41: Warren Spahn, Gaylord Perry, Jim Kaat or Phil Niekro?

126. What was unique about Bill Stoneman's no-hitter against the Mets?

127. Name the six pitchers who threw no-hitters against the Mets.

128. Which hurler was the victim of Dave Kingman's 300th home run?

129. Who hit two homers in the same inning against the Mets?

130. Who is the only player to get a base hit for the Mets and the Montreal Expos on the same day?

131. Whose 8th-inning single broke up Nolan Ryan's bid for a sixth no-hitter?

132. Who hit 59 homers (more than anyone else) against the Mets?

133. The Mets had four players named Miller. Give the first names and their positions.

134. Who was the first Mets regular to be born after the Mets came into existence?
135. On the 1983 club, which three Mets had the same initials?

Miscellaneous—Questions

136. During 1984, which team beat the Mets eight times by only one run?

137. Other than Rusty Staub, who was the only player in major league history to homer as a teenager and as a 40-year-old?

138. What was unusual about the Mets first four games of 1985?

139. Which Met once worked as a department store detective?

140. Who spent seven seasons at Tidewater before making his big-league debut at age 29?

141. Who shaved Darryl Strawberry's head?

142. When Lee Mazzilli returned to the Mets in August 1986, who was wearing his old uniform number?

143. Which Giants pitcher beat the Mets four straight times in 1986?

144. What coincidences occurred when the Mets won their 100th game in 1969 and their 100th game in 1986?

145. What was the Mets record against the Pirates in 1986?

Miscellaneous—Questions

146. When the 1986 World Series began at Shea, which Red Sox player received the loudest ovation?

Answers

1. Ed Charles

2. Tug McGraw

3. Mike Jorgensen

4. Number 21

5. Number 36

6. Number 15

7. Number 11

8. Daniel

Miscellaneous—Answers

9. Among others, Ron Hodges, Mike Howard and Howard Johnson.

10. Wally Backman

11. Ed Glynn

12. Mark Bomback and Charlie Puleo

13. Four

14. Jack Fisher

15. Rod Kanehl, Willie Montanez and Rusty Staub

16. Pitcher Gary Gentry and catcher Jerry Grote—October 6; and pitcher Ron Taylor and catcher J.C. Martin—December 13

17. Ron Taylor

18. Gus Bell and Yogi Berra

19. Paul Siebert and Del Unser

20. John Milner

21. 17

22. 1944

23. Stork

Miscellaneous—Answers

24. Clarence Coleman

25. Chuck, Bob (Hawk), Ron and Sammy

26. Jack Hamilton, Al Jackson and Dennis Musgraves

27. Mookie Wilson

28. Tom Seaver

29. Lee Mazzilli

30. Lee Mazzilli

31. George Weiss

32. John Stearns

33. All are 6 feet 5 inches tall.

34. Doug Flynn

35. Ken MacKenzie

36. 100 to 1

37. William Eckert

38. John Stearns

39. Joe Frazier

Miscellaneous—Answers

40. Paul Siebert

41. Tommie Agee and Cleon Jones

42. Mickey Lolich

43. Tug McGraw (Phillies) defeated Jeff Reardon (Expos)

44. Billy and Rick Baldwin

45. Bud Harrelson

46. Tommy Hall

47. Jesus Alou

48. Jon Matlack

49. Roy Staiger

50. Mrs. Joan Payson

51. The New York Giants

52. Tommie Agee

53. Cleon Jones

54. Ken Boswell, Jerry Grote, Al Jackson and Nolan Ryan

55. Jack Fisher

Miscellaneous—Answers

56. Tracy Stallard

57. Felix the Cat

58. Johnny Vander Meer

59. Donn Clendenon

60. 280 feet down the leftfield line; 258 feet down the rightfield line; and 475 feet to dead center

61. Warren Spahn

62. Gil Hodges

63. Jerry Koosman

64. Tom Seaver and Dick Selma

65. The Dodgers

66. Frank

67. Kevin Collins, then Bobby Pfeil

68. Bing Devine

69. Bob and Don Shaw

70. Bob Miller and Bob Miller

71. Ed Kranepool

Miscellaneous—Answers

72. Joseph Clifton Martin

73. Wayne Garrett was 21 years of age

74. The Mets have played 19 World Series games.

75. Ron Swoboda

76. Sandy Koufax

77. They each had consecutive-game playing streaks of at least 500 games.

78. Jesus Alou

79. Four

80. Bob Aspromonte, Ken Boyer, Sammy Drake, Wayne Garrett, Bobby Klaus, Joe Torre and Alex Trevino had brothers in the majors.

81. Although they won over 400 games between them, none ever won a game for the Mets.

82. The Cubs, 4-3

83. Rod Kanehl (also known as "Hot Rod")

84. The game marked the 11th victory in a row for the Dodgers and the 11th straight loss for the Mets.

Miscellaneous—Answers

85. At the time, number 14 was worn by Gil Hodges.

86. Lou Brock and Hank Aaron hit homers into the Polo Grounds' bleachers on successive days.

87. Marvin (Eugene) Throneberry

88. Marv Throneberry

89. Elio Chacon (1962)

90. Charlie Neal

91. Jay Hook

92. Stan Musial (July 8, 1962)

93. Craig wore number 13 for a time during the losing streak. He went back to number 38 after he won.

94. Al Jackson

95. Dodgers won 44; Mets won 6.

96. 1965

97. Donn Clendenon

98. Five Mets catchers wore number 5: Chris Cannizzaro, Francisco Estrada, Hobie

Miscellaneous—Answers

Landrith, Joe Pignatano and Norm Sherry

99. After being hit on the right arm by a pitch (while batting left-handed), Selma decided to bat right-handed only, with his left side facing the pitcher and right side (and arm) hidden from view.

100. Willie McCovey

101. 1963

102. Billy Williams

103. The Astros scored 11 runs in the top of the 9th inning in the first game of a double-header, and 10 runs in the third inning of the second game.

104. Wilmer "Vinegar Bend" Mizell

105. Reggie Jackson

106. Wade Blasingame

107. Willie McCovey, Willie Stargell and Henry Aaron

108. Jim Beauchamp (1972). The Mets won that game and the next by identical 4-2 scores. In the two contests, Beauchamp drove in seven of their eight runs.

Miscellaneous—Answers

109. Tommy Hutton

110. Tim Foli

111. Jim Beauchamp

112. Lee Mazzilli

113. The Mets beat Carlton four times (1972) although no other team beat him more than once.

114. Marty Perez

115. Juan Marichal

116. The Cincinnati Reds

117. Don Gullett

118. Bob Miller

119. He resigned.

120. Woody Fryman pitched one-hitters against the Mets in 1966 and 1975.

121. Power failure! A citywide blackout had brought New York to a halt.

122. Jack Fisher

123. Rube Walker

Miscellaneous—Answers

124. Sutton's 209th career win tied Don Drysdale's club record.

125. Jim Kaat

126. Stoneman's classic was the first major league no-hitter pitched outside the United States.

127. Sandy Koufax (1962), Jim Bunning (1964), Jim Maloney* (1965), Bob Moose (1969), Bill Stoneman (1972) and Ed Halicki (1975) pitched no-hitters against the Mets.

    *Maloney pitched no-hit ball for 10 innings but lost the no-hitter and the game in the 11th on Johnny Lewis's home run.

128. Rich Gale of the Giants

129. Ray Knight hit a solo shot and a grand-slammer in the same inning against the Mets. In 1985, Von Hayes did the same.

130. Joel Youngblood singled for both teams on the day he was traded (August 4, 1982).

131. Ron Hodges

132. Willie Stargell

133. Bob G., Bob L., Dyar and Larry Miller were all pitchers.

Miscellaneous—Answers

134. Jose Oquendo

135. Jose Oquendo, Jesse Orosco and Junior Ortiz

136. The San Francisco Giants

137. Ty Cobb

138. The Mets won all four by one run.

139. Doug Sisk

140. Rick Anderson

141. Kevin Mitchell

142. Dwight Gooden (16)

143. Mike Krukow

144. Both games took place in Chicago; both times the losing pitcher was a former Met—Dick Selma in 1969 and Ed Lynch in 1986.

145. Mets won 17 and lost 1.

146. Tom Seaver